Recipes by Wm. A. Pizzico,
Gina Marie Corporation

Modern Publishing
A Division of Unisystems, Inc.
New York, New York 10022

Printed in Canada

INTRODUCTION

Convenient Cooking™ is just what the modern cook ordered for quick, easy and delicious food.

Whether you are preparing a simple meal for one, an intimate dinner for two, or a banquet for family or friends, the **Convenient Cooking**™ series will take the work out of planning and preparing your menus, enabling you to enjoy the occasion and the food!

Eight exciting titles provide a convenient recipe center of easy-to-handle, easy-to-read books for every cooking need: meats and ground meats; seafood; chicken and poultry; soups, salads and sauces; omelettes, casseroles and vegetables; microwave meals; desserts; and Cajun food.

Whether you are a beginning cook, or a seasoned food preparer, you will delight in choosing from the range of basic, traditional fare to exotic meals that this series has to offer.

Welcome to the enjoyable and delicious world of **Convenient Cooking**.™

AMBROSIA

Ingredients:

2 pints sour cream
2 (11 ounce) cans
   mandarin oranges,
   sliced
1/2 package (10 1/2
   ounces) miniature
   marshmallows
1 small bag shredded
   coconut
1 (3 1/2 ounce) box
   instant pistachio
   pudding

Directions:

Mix all ingredients together. Refrigerate before serving.

Serves: 7-10

AMBROSIA DELIGHT

Ingredients:

1 pound bag miniature
   marshmallows
2 small cans mandarin
   oranges
1 large can pineapple
   chunks
1 (9 ounce) bag shredded
   coconut
2 ounces slivered
   almonds
Small jar maraschino
   cherries, sliced
1 pint light cream

Directions:

Put marshmallows in a bowl, drain fruit and add to bowl. Add coconut and almonds next, pour light cream over this and mix. Place in the refrigerator overnight. Place sliced cherries on top of mixture and serve.

Serves: 8-10

APEAS CAKES

Ingredients:
- 4 cups flour
- 2 teaspoons baking powder
- 2 sticks margarine
- 2 cups brown sugar
- 1 teaspoon baking soda
- 1 cup cold water

Directions:
Work flour, baking powder, baking soda, margarine and brown sugar together like pie dough. Add water gradually; dough will be sticky. Press dough evenly onto bottoms and sides of 2 (9-inch) pie dishes that have been greased and floured. Scratch dough with fork before baking and sprinkle with granulated sugar. Bake at 350°F for 30 to 40 minutes.

Serves: 8-10

APPLE BREAD PUDDING

Ingredients:
- 5 eggs
- 1 1/2 cans evaporated milk
- 3 cups milk
- 1/2 cup sugar
- 1 teaspoon cinnamon
- 1 teaspoon vanilla
- 5 slices white bread, cut into cubes
- 3 large MacIntosh apples, peeled and cut
- 3 tablespoons butter

Directions:
Beat eggs, add evaporated milk, milk, sugar, vanilla, cinnamon, bread cubes and apples. Mix well. Turn into a shallow baking dish that is well buttered. Dot with butter and bake 450°F for 45 minutes. Pudding is done when a knife inserted comes out clean.

Serves: 4-6

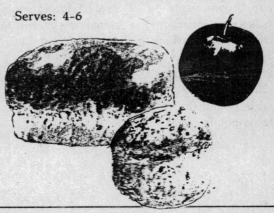

APPLE COBBLER

Ingredients:
1/2 cup butter
3 cups apples, peeled and sliced
3/4 cup sugar
3/4 teaspoon salt
1/2 cup milk
1 egg
1 1/2 cups flour
2 teaspoons baking powder

Directions:
Melt 4 tablespoons butter and pour into an 8-inch square pan. Spread evenly and spread apples over top. Mix 1/4 teaspoon salt with 1/4 cup sugar. Sprinkle over apples. Set aside. Melt remaining butter in saucepan. Remove from heat. Add milk and egg. Beat well. Mix flour, baking powder, remaining sugar and salt in bowl. Stir in milk and egg mixture. With mixer, mix 2 minutes on medium speed. Pour over apples. Bake in a 375°F oven for 30 minutes or until toothpick comes out clean.

Serves: 6

APPLE CRISP PIE

Ingredients:
2 cups oatmeal
1 cup flour
3/4 cup butter
1 cup brown sugar
1 teaspoon cinnamon
5 thinly sliced baking apples, peeled
1 tablespoon lemon juice
2 tablespoons flour
2 tablespoons sugar

Directions:
Combine first 5 ingredients, reserve 1 cup of this mixture, press remainder into a 9-inch pie plate. Toss apples with lemon, flour and sugar. Mound apples in pie shell and top with remaining crumb mixture. Bake at 350°F for 35 to 40 minutes.

Serves: 6

APPLE CRUNCH

Ingredients:
6 to 8 apples, peeled and sliced
1/2 cup water
1 1/2 teaspoons cinnamon
1/2 cup butter
1 cup sugar
3/4 cup flour

Directions:
Butter a casserole dish, and add apples. Pour water over apples and sprinkle with cinnamon. In a bowl, mix butter, sugar and flour until mixture forms crumbs. Sprinkle mixture over apples and bake uncovered at 350°F for 1 hour.

Serves: 6-8

APRICOT BRANDY POUNDCAKE

Ingredients:
1 cup butter
3 cups sugar
6 eggs
1 cup sour cream
1/2 cup apricot brandy
1 teaspoon vanilla
1/2 teaspoon rum extract
1 teaspoon orange extract
1/2 teaspoon almond extract
1/2 teaspoon lemon extract
3 cups flour
1/2 teaspoon baking soda
1/2 teaspoon salt

Directions:
Cream butter and add sugar. Add eggs and beat thoroughly. Combine the next seven ingredients in a separate bowl. Sift together flour, baking soda and salt. Add flour and sour cream mixtures, alternately, to the sugar mixture. Mix well until blended. Pour into a greased and floured bundt pan. Bake at 325°F for 1 1/2 hours. When toothpick comes out clean, cake is done.

Serves: 8-10.

APPLE NUT SQUARES

Ingredients:
2 cups flour
2 cups sugar
2 teaspoons baking soda
1/2 teaspoon salt
1 teaspoon cinnamon
1/2 teaspoon nutmeg
4 cups finely diced
apples
1/2 cup softened
margarine
1/2 cup chopped pecans
2 eggs
Confectioner's sugar

Directions:
Combine flour, sugar, baking soda, salt, cinnamon and nutmeg. Add the apples, margarine, pecans and eggs and beat until just combined. Turn into greased 9 x 13 inch pan and spread evenly. Bake at 325°F for 50 minutes. Cut into squares. Top with confectioner's sugar just before serving.

Serves: 10-12

APPLE OR PEACH CRISP

Ingredients:
4 cups sliced apples
3/4 teaspoon nutmeg
3/4 cup brown sugar,
packed
1/2 cup rolled oats
3/4 teaspoon cinnamon
1/3 cup soft butter
1/2 cup flour

Directions:
Heat oven to 375°F. Place fruit in greased 8-inch square pan or 10 x 6 x 1 1/2-inch oblong baking dish. Blend remaining ingredients until mixture is crumbly. Spread over fruit. Bake 30 to 35 minutes or until fruit is tender and topping is golden brown. Serve warm with ice cream. *Helpful Hints:* If using canned fruit, use a 1 pound, 13 ounce can and 2/3 cup brown sugar.

Serves: 6

APRICOT DELIGHT BARS

Ingredients:
1 1/2 cups sifted flour
1 teaspoon baking
  powder
1/4 teaspoon salt
1 1/2 cups oatmeal
1 cup brown sugar
3/4 cup butter
3/4 cup apricot
  preserves

Directions:
Sift together flour, baking powder and salt. Stir in oats and sugar. Cut in butter until crumbly. Pack two-thirds of the mixture into an 11 x 7 x 1 1/2-inch pan and spread with preserves. Cover with remaining mixture. Bake at 350°F for 35 minutes or until brown. Cool. Cut into bars.

Serves: 10

BANANA BREAD

Ingredients:
3 to 4 bananas, very
  ripe
2 eggs, beaten
3/4 cup sugar
2 cups flour
1 teaspoon baking soda
1 teaspoon salt
1/2 cup walnuts,
  chopped fine
2 tablespoons cooking
  oil

Directions:
In bowl, mash bananas with fork until creamy. Add eggs and sugar to bowl and mix well. Stir in flour, baking soda and salt. With electric mixer, beat 2 minutes. Stir in nuts. Coat loaf pan with cooking oil and pour batter into pan. Bake in 325°F oven for 1 hour. Let cool 20 minutes before removing from pan. *Helpful Hints:* Try crushing walnuts by placing in a baggy and rolling with rolling pin. This brings out flavor of walnuts better than when chopped.

Serves: 8

BANANA-PINEAPPLE CAKE

Ingredients:
3 cups flour
2 teaspoons baking soda
1 teaspoon cinnamon
1 1/2 cup oil
1 teaspoon vanilla
1 cup crushed pineapple
   with juice
1 1/2 cup sugar
1 teaspoon salt
3 large bananas
3 large eggs

Directions:
Mix all ingredients until blended. Do not beat. Pour into a 10-inch tube pan that has been greased and floured and bake at 350°F for 1 hour and 10 minutes.

Serves: 10-12

BLUEBERRY MUFFINS

Ingredients:
2 cups flour
1/2 cup sugar
3 teaspoons baking
   powder
1/2 teaspoon salt
1 cup milk
1 egg, beaten
3 tablespoons butter or
   margarine
1 cup fresh blueberries

Directions:
Mix dry ingredients. Add milk and egg. Stir with fork until thoroughly mixed. Coat muffin tins with butter or margarine. Fold blueberries into batter. Spoon into tins, two-thirds full. Bake 15 minutes at 400°F.

Serves: 12

BLUEBERRY CAKE

Ingredients:

Cake:

2 cups blueberries
Juice from 1/2 lemon
3/4 cup sugar
3 tablespoons
   shortening
1/2 cup milk
1 cup flour
1 teaspoon baking
   powder
1/4 teaspoon salt
1 teaspoon cinnamon

Topping:

1/2 cup sugar
1 tablespoon cornstarch
1/4 teaspoon salt

Directions:

For topping: mix together all topping ingredients and set aside. *For cake:* place blueberries in well-greased 8x8x2 inch pan. Sprinkle lemon juice over berries. Blend flour, baking powder, salt and cinnamon. Cream sugar and shortening, then add milk and flour mixture, alternately. Spread evenly over berries. Sprinkle topping over cake. Bake at 350°F for 45 to 50 minutes. Serve warm.

Serves: 8

BLUEBERRY CRUMB CAKE

Ingredients:

Topping:
1/4 cup sugar
1 1/2 teaspoon cinnamon
3/4 cup flour
1/4 cup melted margarine

Cake:
1/2 cup margarine
3/4 cup sugar
1 egg
1/3 cup milk
2 cups flour
2 teaspoons baking powder
1/2 teaspoon salt
1 tablespoon grated lemon rind
2 cans (21 ounces) blueberry pie filling

Directions:

For topping: mix together topping ingredients until mixture is crumbly. *For cake:* cream margarine and sugar. Add egg and milk. Mix thoroughly. Add remaining ingredients except fruit filling, and blend well. Pour half of batter into greased 9x12-inch baking dish. Spread fruit filling over batter. Pour rest of batter over fruit. Crumble topping over batter. Bake at 350°F for 45 minutes.

Serves: 8-10

BREAD PUDDING

Ingredients:

2 eggs, well beaten
1/2 cup sugar
2 cups milk
1/4 teaspoon ground nutmeg
3 cups soft bread cubes
1/2 cup raisins

Directions:

Beat the sugar, milk and nutmeg into the eggs. Butter a 1 1/2-quart baking dish. Put bread cubes into dish and pour egg mixture over bread. Let stand until bread is thoroughly soaked. Mix in the raisins. Bake at 350°F about 25 minutes. Serve warm.

Serves: 4

YELLOW CAKE

Ingredients:

Cake:
3 eggs
2/3 cup shortening
1 1/2 cups sugar
2 1/4 cups flour
2 1/2 teaspoons baking
  powder
1 teaspoon salt
1 cup milk
1 1/2 teaspoons vanilla
Icing:
1/2 stick butter
2/3 box confectioner's
  sugar
1/8 cup milk

Directions:

For cake: cream together the shortening and 1 1/2 cups sugar. Beat the eggs and add to the mixture. Sift together the flour, baking powder and salt. Stir in, alternately, the 1 cup of milk, the vanilla, and the flour mixture. Bake in 2 greased and floured 9-inch pans at 350°F for 25 to 30 minutes. *For icing:* cream the 1/2 stick butter with the confectioner's sugar and milk. Add more or less sugar and milk to desired consistency.

Serves: 12

CHOCOLATE DIPPED STRAWBERRIES

Ingredients:
1 pint strawberries
  (leave stems intact)
6 ounces semisweet
  chocolate chips
2 tablespoons water
2 tablespoons oil

Directions:
Rinse strawberries and set aside to dry. Place chips in top of double boiler. Allow water on bottom of double boiler to become hot, but do not let it boil. Add water and oil to chips. As they melt, stir until smooth. Holding stem of strawberry, dip in chocolate. Set on wax paper and refrigerate for 1/2 hour.

Serves: 6

CARROT PUDDING CAKE

Ingredients:
1 1/2 cups shortening
1 cup brown sugar
4 eggs, separated
2 1/2 cups flour
1 teaspoon baking
  powder
1 teaspoon baking soda
1 teaspoon salt
2 teaspoon vanilla
1/2 cup water
1 teaspoon lemon juice
2 cups raw carrots,
  finely grated
1 cup chopped walnuts

Directions:
Cream shortening with brown sugar. Add egg yolks, flour, baking powder, baking soda, salt, vanilla, water and lemon juice. Beat thoroughly. Beat egg whites until they peak. Fold beaten egg whites into shortening-flour mixture. Add carrots and walnuts. Mix until well blended. Bake in a well-greased, 10-inch tube pan at 350°F for 45 minutes to 1 hour.

Serves: 12.

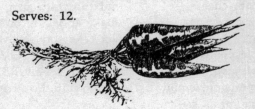

CHEESECAKE I

Ingredients:
- 4 egg whites, beaten very stiff
- 1 cup granulated sugar
- 1 teaspoon vanilla
- 1 1/2 pounds (24 ounces) cream cheese
- 2 cups crushed zweiback crumbs
- 1 pint sour cream
- 1/2 cup sugar
- 1/2 teaspoon vanilla

Directions:

Cream 1 cup of sugar, the cream cheese, and 1 teaspoon vanilla together. Mix in egg whites. Grease 9-inch springform pan with butter. Press zweiback crumbs into pan, but reserve some for topping. Fill pan with mixture. Bake at 350°F for 25 minutes or until top starts to crack. Remove from oven, turn up to 425°F. Mix the sour cream, the 1/2 cup sugar, and 1/2 teaspoon vanilla. Beat lightly. Pour over top of cake, and sprinkle with zwieback crumbs. Put back in the oven for 5 minutes.

Serves: 12-15

CHEESECAKE II

Ingredients:
- 1 pint sour cream
- 1 1/2 pounds (3 cups) ricotta cheese
- 2 (8 ounce) packages cream cheese
- 1 1/2 cups sugar
- 6 eggs
- 6 tablespoons flour
- 1 tablespoon vanilla
- 1 tablespoon lemon juice
- 1 teaspoon cinnamon

Directions:

Cream sour cream, cheeses, and sugar together. Beat in eggs one at a time. Mix in flour, then add vanilla and lemon juice. Grease and flour an 8-inch springform pan. Pour mixture into pan. Sprinkle with cinnamon. Bake at 350°F for 1 hour. Turn off oven but let cake stay in oven for an extra hour. DO NOT OPEN OVEN DOOR FOR THE ENTIRE 2 HOURS. (This cake is best if you let it set in the refrigerator for 12 to 24 hours.)

Serves: 12

CHEESECAKE CUPCAKES

Ingredients:
3 (8 ounce) packages
   cream cheese
5 eggs, separated
1 cup sugar
1/4 teaspoon salt
1 teaspoon vanilla
1 cup heavy cream,
   whipped (optional)
Cherries (optional)

Directions:
Soften cream cheese in bowl. Add egg yolks, sugar, salt and vanilla. Beat 3 minutes. In another bowl, beat egg whites into peaks. Fold them into the cheese mixture. Pour mixture into miniature, foil baking cups. Bake at 325°F for 20 minutes. Cracks will form on top. Cool and top with whipped cream and cherries.

Serves: 24

CHEESECAKE PARFAITS

Ingredients:
4 cups miniature
   marshmallows
1/4 cup milk
2 (8 ounce) packages
   cream cheese,
   softened
1/4 cup brandy
1 cup heavy cream,
   whipped
4 cups canned or frozen
   fruit, drained
   (peaches, blueberries
   and strawberries.)

Directions:
Melt marshmallows with milk in top of double boiler. Stir until smooth. Chill until thickened. Combine softened cream cheese and brandy, beating until well blended and fluffy. Whip in marshmallow mixture; fold in whipped cream. Chill. For each parfait, layer 1/2 cup mixture alternately with 1/2 cup fruit in parfait glass.

Serves: 8

CHERRY CHEESE CHARLOTTE

Ingredients:
1 cup chilled evaporated milk
1/4 cup fresh lemon juice
1 tablespoon grated lemon rind
1 cup heavy cream
1/2 cup sour cream
1/2 cup superfine sugar
1 (1 pound, 5 ounce) can cherry pie filling
Split 24 lady fingers in half lengthwise (to be used to line the sides and bottom of 8-inch spring form pan)

Directions:
In large bowl, beat evaporated milk, lemon juice and rind at high speed until very foamy and slightly thick. In small bowl, beat heavy cream until very stiff. Fold into whipped milk-lemon mixture along with sugar and sour cream. Pour into pan lined with lady fingers. Chill at least 4 hours. Use slotted spoon to drain fruit. Top cheese charlotte with drained fruit. Reserve syrup to use as sauce. Chill 30 minutes. Gently loosen with spatula.

Serves: 8

CHERRY PUDDING

Ingredients:
1/2 cup butter, room temperature
2/3 cup sugar
4 eggs
3/4 cup ground almonds
1 teaspoon grated lemon peel
1 cup crushed vanilla wafers
2 cups cream
2 cups black bing cherries, drained and pitted

Directions:
Cream butter and sugar until light and fluffy. Separate eggs. Add yolks to butter and sugar mixture. Reserve whites. Add almonds, vanilla wafer crumbs, and 1 cup cream, mixing well. Beat egg whites until they peak, and fold into batter. Pour half of batter into a well-buttered, 8-inch casserole dish and bake at 350°F for 15 minutes. Remove from oven and cover pudding with cherries. Pour remaining batter over cherries and continue baking 20 minutes or until firm. Serve with remaining cream.

Serves: 4-6

CHOCOLATE BREAD PUDDING

Ingredients:
1 1/2 squares
   unsweetened
   chocolate, cut into
   pieces
3 cups cold milk
1/2 teaspoon salt
1/2 cup sugar
3 eggs, slightly beaten
1 teaspoon vanilla
2 cups bread cubes

Directions:
Add chocolate to milk in top of double boiler and heat. When chocolate is melted, beat with egg beater. Combine sugar, salt and eggs and vanilla. Add to milk mixture and pour over bread in baking dish. Bake for 1/2 hour at 400°F.

Serves: 12

CHOCOLATE CAKE

Ingredients:

4 squares chocolate (4 ounces) melted
1 cup boiling water
2 cups granulated sugar
2 cups cake flour
1/2 teaspoon salt
1 1/2 teaspoons baking soda
1/2 cup sour milk
2 eggs
1 teaspoon vanilla

Directions:

Combine all ingredients, mixing well. Bake at 350°F for 30 minutes in a greased, 10-inch tube pan.

Serves: 12-15

CHOCOLATE CHIP CAKE

Ingredients:

Cake:
1/4 cup butter
1 cup sugar
2 eggs
1 cup sour cream
1 teaspoon vanilla
2 cups flour
1 1/2 teaspoons baking powder
1 teaspoon baking soda
Chip mixture:
1 cup chocolate chips
1/2 cup sugar
1 teaspoon cinnamon

Directions:

For chip mixture: Combine all chip mixture ingredients. *For cake:* cream butter, sugar and eggs. Add sour cream and vanilla. Add dry ingredients and beat. Pour half of batter into a greased 13 x 9 x 2 inch oblong pan. Spoon half of chip mixture over the top. Pour remaining batter on top and spread with a wet knife. Then put remaining chip mixture on top. Bake at 350°F for 30 to 35 minutes.

Serves: 8-10

BROWNIES

Ingredients:
1 cup sugar
1/2 cup margarine or butter
4 eggs
1 teaspoon vanilla
1 (2 pound) can chocolate syrup
1 cup plus 1 tablespoon flour
1/2 teaspoon baking powder
1/4 teaspoon salt
3/4 cup chopped walnuts (optional)

Directions:
Beat sugar and margarine or butter until light. Beat in eggs, two at a time, then add vanilla. Stir in syrup. Stir in flour, baking powder and salt. Then add nuts. Pour into a greased and floured, 9 x 9 x 2 inch pan and bake at 350°F for 20-25 minutes.

Serves: 12

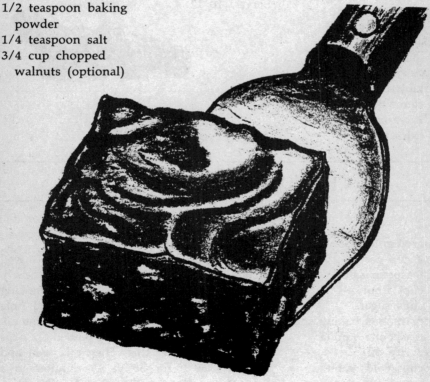

CHOCOLATE RAISIN CAKE

Ingredients:
Cake:
1 1/2 cups cold water
1 cup sugar
1/2 cup margarine
1 cup raisins
1/2 teaspoon cinnamon
1/2 teaspoon cloves
2 squares chocolate
1/2 cup flour
1 teaspoon baking soda
1/4 teaspoon salt
1 teaspoon vanilla
Icing:
1 (8 ounce) package
    cream cheese
2 tablespoons
    confectioner's sugar
1/2 teaspoon almond
    extract

Directions:
For cake: boil water, sugar, margarine, raisins, cinnamon, cloves and chocolate. Cool. Dissolve baking soda in 2 tablespoons of cold water and add to cooled mixture. Add salt, flour and vanilla. Blend well. Pour into a greased and floured, 9-inch square pan. Bake 350°F for 35 minutes. Cool. *For Icing:* combine all icing ingredients and spread icing over cooled cake.

Serves: 10-12

CHOCOLATE WACKY CAKE

Ingredients:
1/2 cup cocoa
1 teaspoon salt
3 cups flour
2 cups sugar
2 teaspoons baking soda
2 teaspoons vanilla
2/3 cup oil
2 cups cold water
2 teaspoons vinegar

Directions:
Mix dry ingredients together until well blended (do all mixing in one large bowl). Make 3 holes in dry ingredients In the first hole place the vinegar, in the second hole place the vanilla, and in the third hole the oil. DO NOT STIR. Immediately pour the 2 cups of cold water over this. Then mix well and bake at 350°F for 35 to 40 minutes in a greased and floured 13 x 9 x 2 inch pan.

Serves: 12-15

CHOCOLATE CHIP PIE

Ingredients:
2 eggs beaten
2 sticks margarine (melted) and cooled to room temperature
1/2 cup flour, sifted
1/2 cup brown sugar
1/2 cup granulated sugar
1 cup chocolate chips
1 cup walnuts, chopped
1 9-inch pie shell, unbaked

Directions:
In bowl, beat eggs; add cooled margarine. Slowly add flour and sugars. Fold in chocolate chips and nuts. Pour into unbaked, 9-inch pie shell. Bake at 325°F for 1 hour.

Serves: 6-8

CLASSIC APPLE CAKE

Ingredients:
1 tablespoon margarine
2 eggs
1/2 cup cooking oil
1/4 cup orange juice
1 teaspoon vanilla
1 cup sugar, plus 2 teaspoons
1/2 teaspoon baking powder
Pinch of salt
1 1/2 cups flour
2 medium cooking apples, peeled, sliced into thin wedges
2 teaspoons cinnamon

Directions:
Coat loaf pan with margarine and set aside. In mixing bowl, combine eggs, cooking oil, orange juice and vanilla. Lightly stir together. Add 1 cup sugar, baking powder, salt and flour. With electric mixer, beat 2 minutes. Pour half of batter into a greased and floured standard-sized loaf pan. Layer half of apple wedges over top. Sprinkle with 1 teaspoon sugar and 2 teaspoons cinnamon. Pour remaining batter over apples. Arrange remaining apples over top and sprinkle with remaining sugar and cinnamon. Bake in 375°F oven 55 minutes or until toothpick comes out clean when poked into center of cake. Cool 20 minutes before removing from pan. *Options:* Before baking sprinkle chopped walnuts or pecans over the apples in center and on the top.

Serves: 12

COOL NECTARINE DESSERT

Ingredients:
4 cups sliced, fresh nectarines
2 tablespoons lemon juice
2 teaspoons sugar
1 pint sour cream
1/4 cup brown sugar

Directions:
Place fruit in 10-inch pie plate. Sprinkle with lemon juice and sugar. Cover completely with sour cream. Sprinkle brown sugar over sour cream. Put under broiler, 6 inches from heat, until brown sugar melts. Chill. Draw off liquid before serving.

Serves: 6

COCOA CHEESECAKE

Ingredients:
2 (8 ounce) packages cream cheese
6 eggs, separated
1 teaspoon vanilla
1 tablespoon orange juice
1 cup heavy cream, whipped
1 square unsweetened chocolate
1 cup sour cream
3 tablespoons sugar
1 teaspoon vanilla
2 cups crushed graham crackers

Directions:
Blend cheese and add yolks, one at a time, beating well. Stir in vanilla and orange juice. Beat whites until stiff and spoon into cheese mixture. Fold in whipped cream. Melt chocolate in separate pot. Lightly grease a 9-inch springform pan and pat the graham cracker crumbs into place. Spoon in one-third of batter, dribble some chocolate on it and swirl around with knife. Repeat until mixture is all used up. Bake at 300°F for 1 hour. Leave in oven 1 hour longer with door closed and oven turned off. Remove. Combine sugar, vanilla and sour cream. Pour evenly over cake. Return to 350°F oven for 10 minutes. Remove, cool and refrigerate.

Serves: 8-10

COCONUT CUSTARD PIE

Ingredients:
5 eggs, slightly beaten
1/4 teaspoon salt
3/4 cup sugar
3 cups of milk, scalded
1/2 teaspoon vanilla
1 cup coconut
Nutmeg

Directions:
Combine eggs, salt and sugar. Add milk and vanilla. Add coconut. Pour into 9-inch pie shell, sprinkle with nutmeg and bake in hot oven at 475° for 10 minutes. Reduce temperature to 350°F-400°F (depending on oven) and bake 30 to 40 minutes longer.

Serves: 6-8

CHERRY UPSIDE DOWN CAKE

Ingredients:
2/3 cup sugar
2 1/2 tablespoons cornstarch
2 1/2 cups drained sour cherries (reserve syrup)
1/3 cup shortening
1/2 cup sugar
1 egg
1 teaspoon grated orange peel
1 3/4 cups flour
1/2 teaspoon salt
2 teaspoons baking powder
1/4 teaspoon baking soda
1/2 cup orange juice
1/4 cup milk

Directions:
Mix sugar and cornstarch. Add cherry syrup and cook until clear. Add cherries, pour into a greased, 8-inch pan. Cream together shortening, sugar and egg. Beat well. Add orange peel, sift in rest of dry ingredients, and add milk and orange juice. Stir well. Pour into pan. Bake at 375°F for 40 minutes. Let stand 10 minutes. Invert on serving plate.

Serves: 6-8

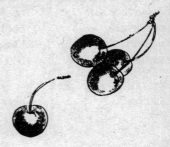

DAINTY LILLIES

Ingredients:

Dough:
1 (8 ounce) package
  cream cheese
1/2 stick butter
2 cups flour
Pinch of salt
Confectioner's sugar
Filling:
1 cup chopped nuts
1/2 cup preserves, any
  flavor

Directions:

For filling: Mix nuts and preserves thoroughly.
For dough: Mix cheese and butter; work in flour and salt. Roll paper thin. Cut into 2-inch squares. Add filling. Roll and fold to shape lily; crimp edges to seal. Bake 15 minutes at 350°F. Powder with confectioner's sugar.

Serves: 3 dozen

DROPPED FILLED COOKIES

Ingredients:

1 cup shortening
2 cups brown sugar
3 eggs
3 1/2 cups flour
1 teaspoon baking soda
1/2 teaspoon salt
1/2 cup water
1 teaspoon vanilla
Pineapple jelly

Directions:

Cream shortening, sugar and eggs together until fluffy. Sift flour, salt and baking soda together. Add to sugar mixture. Add water and vanilla and mix thoroughly. Drop by tablespoonfuls, 2 inches apart, on greased cookie sheet. Make a well in center of each cookie and fill with a teaspoonful of jelly. Drop a half teaspoonful of dough on top of filled cookie. Bake at 375°F for 10 to 12 minutes.

Serves: 3 dozen

EASY CHOCOLATE CHEESE PIE

Ingredients:
1 9-inch graham cracker crust
2 (6 ounce) packages semisweet chocolate morsels
2 (8 ounce) packages cream cheese, softened
1 (14 ounce) can sweetened condensed milk
1 tablespoon vanilla extract

Directions:
Melt chocolate over hot water. Combine cheese, milk and vanilla. Blend in chocolate. Pour into crust and chill overnight or about 4 hours.

Serves: 6-8

FESTIVE JELLO MOLD

Ingredients:
1 3/4 cup water
1 (3 ounce) package orange gelatin
1/2 cup crushed pineapple, drained well
1/4 cup carrots, shredded

Directions:
Boil half of the water. Add gelatin and stir. Remove from heat and add remaining water. Continue stirring until gelatin dissolves. Pour into bowl and refrigerate 1 hour, or until gelatin is three-quarters firm. Remove from refrigerator. With spoon, stir gelatin, adding pineapple and carrots. Stir well and pour into small mold. Return to refrigerator until completely firm. Remove from mold by setting mold in hot water, 1/2 inch from top rim. Place a plate over top and immediately invert the mold onto the plate.

Serves: 4

FLUFFY NESSELRODE PIE

Ingredients:
1 (8 ounce) package
    cream cheese,
    softened
1 cup milk, divided
2 tablespoons light rum
1 (3 3/4 ounce) package
    vanilla instant
    pudding mix
3/4 cup finely chopped
    mixed candied fruits
1 (12 ounce) container
    frozen whipped
    topping (thawed and
    divided)
Chocolate-coconut crust,
    or any pre-baked
    crust

Directions:
Beat cream cheese on low speed of electric mixer until light and fluffy. Gradually add 1/2 cup milk, beating smooth. Add remaining milk, rum and pudding mix. Beat on low speed of mixer until thickened. Let stand 3 minutes. Fold in candied fruit and 3 cups whipped topping. Spoon into chocolate-coconut crust. Chill at least 4 hours. Garnish with remaining whipped topping, and sprinkle with chocolate curls if desired.

Serves: 6

FRESH APPLE CAKE

Ingredients:
3/4 cup cooking oil
2 cups sugar
2 large eggs
2 tablespoon vanilla
3 cups sifted flour
1 1/2 teaspoon baking
    soda
1 teaspoon salt
1 cup chopped walnuts
    or pecans
3 cups chopped,
    unpeeled apples

Directions:
Mix oil, sugar, eggs and vanilla and add to dry ingredients. Mix in nuts and apples. Batter will be stiff and crumbly. Spoon into a well-greased, 10-inch tube pan. Bake at 350°F for 70 minutes. Cool in pan for 10 minutes before turning onto a rack to cool.

Serves: 12

FRESH FRUITS IN SPICY SAUCE

Ingredients:

1 pineapple
1/2 pound seedless Thompson grapes
1 pint strawberries
2 tablespoons sugar
1 cup orange juice
1/3 cup sugar
1 tablespoon lemon juice
2 tablespoons rum
1 tablespoon minced, crystallized ginger
1 pint blueberries

Directions:

Peel, core and quarter the pineapple. Cut each quarter in half, lengthwise. Cut into fan-shaped slices. Rinse and slice the grapes in half and add to the pineapple. Rinse and hull the strawberries and slice in half. Put the strawberries into a separate bowl, sprinkle with 2 tablespoons sugar, and chill. In a small saucepan, mix orange juice with 1/3 cup of sugar and lemon juice. Bring to a boil, lower heat, and simmer for 20 minutes. Remove from heat. Stir in rum and ginger. Add the sauce to the pineapple and grapes. Chill 3 hours. Add the blueberries and the strawberries and their juices just before serving.

Serves: 6-8

ICED PUMPKIN CAKE

Ingredients:

Cake:
4 eggs
2 cups sugar
1 cup oil
2 cups flour
2 teaspoons baking soda
1/2 teaspoon vanilla
1/2 teaspoon salt
2 teaspoons cinnamon
1 cup pumpkin pie mix
1/2 cup raisins
1 cup crushed walnuts

Icing:
2 1/2 cups confectioner's sugar
1/4 teaspoons vanilla
1 (3 ounce) package cream cheese, softened
4 tablespoons butter

Directions:

Mix eggs, sugar and oil. Beat thoroughly. Add flour, baking soda, vanilla, salt, cinnamon and pie mix. Beat well. Add raisins and walnuts. Pour into 10-inch, greased tube pan. Bake 325°F for 1 hour. Cool completely. Mix icing ingredients and spread on cake.

Serves: 8-10

GRANOLA CAKE

Ingredients:
1 1/2 cups boiling water
1 cup natural cereal (plain or raisin)
1 cup white sugar
1 cup brown sugar
1/2 cup shortening
2 eggs
1 teaspoon allspice
1 teaspoon baking soda
1 1/2 cups sifted flour
Confectioner's sugar

Directions:

Lightly grease and flour a 9-inch tube pan. Pour water over cereal and let it stand for 10 minutes. Mix white sugar, brown sugar, shortening, eggs, allspice and baking soda. Add cereal and flour. Pour into tube pan. Bake in 375°F oven for 50 to 55 minutes. Dust top with confectioner's sugar before serving or serve warm with whipped cream.

Serves: 16

FRUIT COCKTAIL CAKE

Ingredients:
Cake:
1/2 cup oil
1 1/2 cup sugar
2 eggs
1/2 cup coconut
2 cups flour
1/2 teaspoon salt
1 1/2 teaspoon baking
   soda
1 medium can fruit
   cocktail
Topping:
1 stick margarine
3/4 cup sugar
1/2 cup evaporated
   milk
1/2 teaspoon vanilla
1/2 cup chopped nuts

Directions:
For cake: mix oil, sugar and eggs. Add juice from cocktail and mix with above ingredients. Add fruit cocktail and all other ingredients, except coconut, together. Mix and pour into ungreased 8 x 10 x 2 inch pan. Sprinkle top with 1/2 cup coconut. Bake at 300°F for 40 minutes. *For topping:* bring first 3 ingredients to a boil and remove from heat. Add 1/2 teaspoon vanilla and 1/2 cup nuts. Pour over cake while cake is hot.

Serves: 9

FUNNEL CAKE

Ingredients:
2 cups flour
1 tablespoon sugar
1 teaspoon baking
   powder
Pinch of salt
1 1/4 cups milk
2 eggs
1/2 cup cooking oil
1/4 cup confectioner's
   sugar

Directions:
Mix dry ingredients. Add milk and eggs. Mix briskly with fork until smooth. Meanwhile heat oil over medium heat in a heavy skillet. Pour batter from spouted measuring cup or container. Pour into hot oil in a zigzag design. Fry 2 minutes or until bottom is golden brown. Carefully turn over and fry 1 minute more. Remove to plate. Sift confectioner's sugar over top.

Serves: 1

FROSTED CARROT CAKE

Ingredients:

Cake:
4 eggs
2 1/2 cups flour
2 tablespoons wheat
  germ
2 cups sugar
2 teaspoons cinnamon
2 teaspoons baking soda
1 teaspoon salt
1 1/2 cups oil
3 jars strained baby
  carrots
1/2 cup chopped nuts
  or raisins (or both)
Icing:
1 (8 ounce) package
  cream cheese
Approximately 2 1/2
  cups powdered sugar
1 teaspoon vanilla

Directions:

For cake: preheat oven to 350°F. Grease and flour 9-inch square pan. In large bowl, beat eggs, carrots, sugar, wheat germ and cinnamon. Combine dry ingredients and add alternately with the oil. Add nuts and/or raisins. Spread into pan. Bake for 50 minutes. Test with toothpick for doneness. *For icing:* beat cheese, sugar and vanilla. Spread on cake.

Serves: 6

INDIVIDUAL CHEESECAKES

Ingredients:

8 ounces cream cheese,
  softened
1/2 cup sugar
1 teaspoon vanilla
2 eggs
Gingersnaps
Cherry pie filling
  (optional)

Directions:

Beat cream cheese, sugar, vanilla and eggs for 5 minutes. Place cupcake papers in muffin tin. Place a gingersnap in the bottom of cup; fill cups halfway. Bake 350°F for 15 minutes. Cool. Top with pie filling if desired.

Serves: 12

LEMON MOUSSE

Ingredients:

1 cup heavy cream
1 small package coconut
1 envelope unflavored gelatin
1/4 cup water
4 eggs, separated
2/3 cup sugar
1/4 cup lemon juice
2 tablespoons lemon rind
Fresh strawberries (optional)

Directions:

Beat cream until stiff, and refrigerate. Toast coconut under broiler until light brown. Cool and set aside. Soften gelatin in water in double boiler or in pan over hot water. Beat egg yolks in a separate bowl. Gradually add sugar and beat until frothy. Beat whites until stiff and set aside. Add lemon juice and rind and gelatin to yolks. Fold in egg whites and beaten cream. Pour half of mixture into 6 individual custard cups. Sprinkle with half of toasted coconut. Pour remaining mixture over coconut. Sprinkle remaining toasted coconut over top. Garnish with fresh strawberries.

Serves: 6

CREAM CHEESE FLUFFY FROSTING

Ingredients:

1 small package cream cheese
3/4 stick margarine
2/3 jar whipped marshmallow
1 pound confectioner's sugar
2 or 3 tablespoons milk

Directions:

Beat cream cheese and margarine until smooth. Add sugar and marshmallow whip alternately with milk. Whip well.

Serves: Frosts one cake

PINEAPPLE LIME SUPREME

Ingredients:
1 (3 ounce) package lime gelatin
1 cup boiling water
1 (3 ounce) package cream cheese
2/3 cup crushed pineapple with juice
1/2 cup celery, finely cut
1/2 cup heavy whipped cream
Maraschino cherries for garnish (optional)

Directions:
Add gelatin to hot water and then add cheese. Beat with rotary beater until well blended. Chill until lightly firm, then add celery and pineapple. Chill a little longer and add the whipped cream, folding lightly. Garnish with maraschino cherries if desired.

Serves: 6

LEMON CAKE

Ingredients:
Cake:
1 can sweetened condensed milk
2 eggs
1/2 cup lemon juice
Lemon rind
1/2 cup flour
Crust:
1 cup graham cracker crumbs, or prepared crust
1/2 teaspoon cinnamon
1/2 teaspoon nutmeg
3 tablespoons brown sugar
3 tablespoons margarine

Directions:
Blend all cake ingredients. Combine all crust ingredients and press into bottom of a 9-inch pie plate. Pour cake ingredients into crust. Bake 10 minutes at 300°F. Cool. Refrigerate. Serve cold.

Serves: 6-8

ORANGE DELIGHT CAKE

Ingredients:

Cake:
1 large orange, pulp
   and peel
1 cup golden raisins
1/3 cup walnuts
2 cups flour
1 teaspoon baking soda
1 teaspoon salt
1 cup sugar
1/2 cup shortening
1 cup milk
2 eggs
Topping:
1/3 cup orange juice
1/3 cup cinnamon
1/4 cup chopped
   walnuts

Directions:

For cake: cut orange in half and squeeze out juice; reserve juice for topping. Grind together orange pulp and peel, raisins and walnuts. Sift together flour, soda, salt and sugar. Add shortening and 3/4 cup milk. Beat thoroughly at medium speed. Add eggs and 1/4 cup milk. Mix well. Fold orange-raisin mixture into batter. Generously grease and flour a 12 x 8 x 2 inch pan. Pour batter into pan. Bake at 350°F for 40 to 50 minutes. *For topping:* drip 1/3 cup orange juice over warm cake. Combine cinnamon and chopped nuts. Sprinkle over cake.

Serves: 8-10

MAGIC COOKIES

Ingredients:
1/2 cup butter
1 1/2 cups graham
   cracker crumbs
1 can condensed milk
   (not evaporated milk)
1 (6 ounce) package
   semisweet chocolate
   chips
1 (3 1/2 ounce) can
   flaked coconut
1 cup chopped nuts

Directions:

In a 13 x 9 inch baking pan, melt butter and then remove from heat. Sprinkle crumbs over butter; pour milk evenly over crumbs. Top with chocolate chips, coconut and nuts and press down gently. Bake at 350°F for 25 minutes, or until golden brown.

Serves: Makes 2 dozen

MY BEST DOUGHNUTS

Ingredients:

2 eggs
1 cup sugar
1 cup milk
1 teaspoon vanilla
4 tablespoons melted butter
4 cups flour
3 teaspoons baking powder

Directions:

Beat the eggs and sugar until light and fluffy. Add the milk, melted butter and vanilla and mix well. Sift flour and baking powder together and add gradually to the mixture. Roll out on a floured board and cut with a doughnut cutter or use a glass and thimble. Fry in hot fat about 350°F (when a cube of bread browns quickly, fat is hot enough). Turn each doughnut, and when lightly fried on both sides remove from fat and drain on paper towels.

Serves: Makes 1 dozen

LEMON COINS

Ingredients:

1 1/2 cups sifted all-purpose flour
1/2 teaspoon baking soda
1/2 teaspoon salt
1/2 cup vegetable shortening
1 cup sugar
1 egg
1 tablespoon lemon juice
1/2 cup finely chopped pecans

Directions:

Measure flour, soda and salt into a sifter. In a medium-sized bowl, cream shortening with sugar until fluffy. Beat in egg, lemon juice and pecans. Sift in flour mixture, blending well to make a soft dough. Shape into 2 long rolls; wrap in wax paper; chill overnight. When ready to bake, slice dough 1/4 inch thick; place on cookie sheets. Bake in moderate oven (375°F) for 8 minutes, or until golden around edges. Remove from cookie sheets; cool completely on wire racks.

Serves: Makes 4 dozen.

PHILLY STRAWBERRY SHORTCAKE

Ingredients:

1-pint strawberries,
  rinsed, stems removed
3/4 cup whipped
  marshmallow
3/4 cup cream cheese,
  room temperature
4 slices pound cake

Directions:

Slice strawberries and set aside. Combine marshmallow and cream cheese in mixing bowl. With mixer, mix on medium speed for 2 minutes. Arrange cake on four individual plates. Spoon strawberries over top. Scoop cream mixture over strawberries. Arrange a few strawberries on top for garnish.

Serves: 4

PEARS PICASSO

Ingredients:

8 firm ripe pears
2 cups miniature
  marshmallows
2 tablespoons milk
1 (8 ounce) package
  cream cheese, soften
2 tablespoons brandy
1/2 cups heavy cream,
  whipped
Chocolate-flavored
  topping for garnish

Directions:

Peel pears and core from the bottom. Place pears in saucepan with enough water to cover. Cover pan and simmer for 20 minutes or until tender; drain. Chill. Melt marshmallows with milk in top of double boiler and stir until smooth. Chill until thickened. Combine softened cream cheese and brandy, beating until well blended and fluffy. Whip in marshmallow mixture, fold in whipped cream. For each serving, place 1/2 cup cream cheese mixture in serving dish. Top with pear. Spoon chocolate-flavored topping over pear before serving.

Serves: 8

LEMON CAKE PIE

Ingredients:

1 cup sugar
1/4 cup flour
1/4 cup melted butter
2 egg yolks
1/8 teaspoon salt
1 cup milk
2 lemons (juice and
  rind)
2 egg whites, beaten
  stiff
1 (9-inch) pie crust,
  unbaked

Directions:

Combine sugar, flour, melted butter, egg yolks, salt and milk and beat until smooth. Add juice and grated lemon rinds. Stir well. Beat egg whites until stiff, but not dry, and fold into mixture. Pour into unbaked pie crust and bake at 450°F for 10 minutes. Reduce heat to 350°F and bake 30 minutes more.

Serves: 6

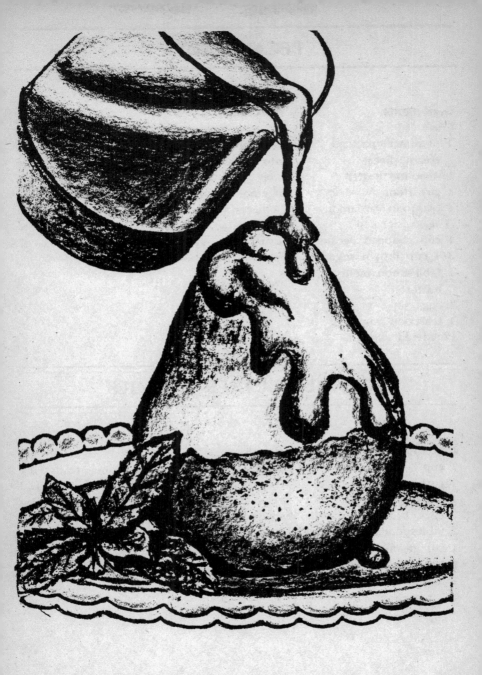

PECAN TARTS

Ingredients:

Crust:
1 (3 ounce) package
   cream cheese
1/4 pound butter
1 cup flour
1 teaspoon cardamon
Filling:
1 cup chopped pecans
3/4 cup brown sugar
1 tablespoon melted
   butter
1 egg
1 teaspoon vanilla
Powdered sugar

Directions:

For crust: cream butter and cream cheese together. Blend in flour and cardamon. Form into ball. Refrigerate until ready to use. *For filling:* add and mix all filling ingredients together. Then take dough and divide it into 24 pieces. Work each piece into a small muffin tin, forming a cup. Add 1 tablespoon filling to each. Bake 375°F for 15 minutes. Cool. Sprinkle with powdered sugar.

Serves: Makes 24 tarts

PEANUT BUTTER COOKIES

Ingredients:

1 cup shortening
1 cup granulated sugar
1 cup brown sugar
2 eggs, beaten
2 tablespoons hot water
1 cup peanut butter
2 1/2 cups flour
1 teaspoon baking soda
1/2 teaspoon salt

Directions:

Cream shortening, add sugars and cream well. Add eggs, hot water and peanut butter. Add dry ingredients to creamed mixture. Drop by tablespoonfuls onto cookie sheets. Bake 350°F for 8 to 10 minutes.

Serves: Makes 2 dozen

GINGERSNAP FRUIT PIE

Ingredients:

About 35 gingersnaps
3 bananas
2 cups applesauce
1 cup frozen orange
   juice concentrate,
   slightly diluted
Margarine
Vanilla ice cream
   (optional)
Whipped cream
   (optional)

Directions:

Grease a 9-inch, deep-dish pie plate. Put 20-24 gingersnap cookies in a blender to make crumbs. Press crumbs to cover bottom of pie plate. Halve enough gingersnaps to place around the rim, the circled part of each cookie half standing up. Slice 3 bananas evenly to cover crumbs. Pour applesauce over bananas. Sprinkle with orange juice. Dot with margarine. Bake 325°F for 45 minutes, or until brown and sticking to the sides. Serve hot with vanilla ice cream or whipped cream.

Serves: 8

STRAWBERRY CHEESE PIE WITH GLAZE

Ingredients:

Crust:
2 cups flour
1 teaspoon baking powder
8 tablespoons sugar
Pinch salt
2 eggs
3/4 cup melted butter

Filling:
1 pound cream cheese
1 cup sugar
4 eggs
4 tablespoons flour
2 teaspoons vanilla
Juice from 1 lemon
12 teaspoons milk

Glaze:
1/2 cup water
2 tablespoons cornstarch
1 pound frozen Strawberries thawed and drained (reserve juice)
2/3 cups juice from strawberries

Directions:

For crust: mix dry ingredients for crust together. Add eggs and butter. Mix with fork. Put into a 13 1/2 x 8 1/2 inch baking dish. Refrigerate. *For the filling:* cream the cheese, add the sugar and blend. Add eggs, one at a time, and blend. Add flour, vanilla and lemon juice and stir. Add milk gradually and mix well. Pour into pie crust. Bake at 325°F for 1 1/4 hours. Sprinkle with cinnamon. *For the glaze:* combine juice from berries, water and cornstarch. Cook until clear and thickened, stirring occasionally; cool in refrigerator. Add strawberries to mixture and spoon over whole pie or each slice as needed.

Serves: 16

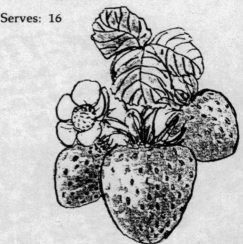

PINEAPPLE-PUDDING SHEET CAKE

Ingredients:

Cake:
1 box yellow cake mix
4 eggs
3/4 cup water
1 package vanilla
  instant pudding

Topping:
6 ounces cream cheese
2 cups milk
2 packages instant
  vanilla pudding
2 large cans pineapple
1 large container non-
  dairy whipped
  topping
1 (9 ounce) bag coconut

Directions:

For cake: mix ingredients for cake together. Grease and flour a 16 1/4 x 11 1/2 x 1 inch cookie sheet. Pour mixture onto cookie sheet and bake at 350°F for 20 minutes. *For topping:* beat cheese, milk and pudding mix until smooth and spread on top of cake. Drain pineapple and spread on top of pudding mixture. Spread container of non-dairy topping over pineapples and then top with coconut.

Serves: 16

PISTACHIO NUT SWIRL CAKE

Ingredients:

1 package yellow cake
  mix
1 package instant
  pistachio pudding mix
4 eggs
1 cup sour cream
1/2 cup oil
1/2 teaspoon almond
  extract
1/2 cup sugar
1 teaspoon cinnamon
1/2 cup chopped,
  shelled pistachios

Directions:

Combine and mix all ingredients except sugar, cinnamon and nuts. Beat for 2 minutes. Pour a third of the batter into a greased bundt or 10-inch tube pan. Mix sugar, nuts and cinnamon. Sprinkle half of this mixture over batter. Repeat layer of batter and sugar, ending with layer of batter. Bake 350°F for 50 minutes.

Serves: 10

BROWN BETTY

Ingredients:
1 cup soft bread
  crumbs
1/2 cup sugar
1/8 teaspoon salt
4 tablespoons melted
  butter
1 1/2 cup sliced apples
1/2 teaspoon cinnamon
1/2 teaspoon vanilla
2/3 cup water

Directions:
Mix all ingredients and pour into buttered baking dish. Cover and bake 30 minutes in a 350°F oven. Remove top and bake 15 minutes to brown. Serve warm. Check occasionally to see if more water is needed.

Serves: 2

RICE PUDDING CAKE

Ingredients:
Butter
6 eggs
1/2 pint sour cream
2 cups cooked rice
2 cups milk
1 cup sugar
1/2 teaspoon nutmeg
1 teaspoon cinnamon

Directions:
Grease a 9 x 13 x 2 inch casserole dish with butter. Combine and mix remaining ingredients. Pour into casserole dish. Bake at 350°F for 30 minutes.

Serves: 10-12

PLANTATION SPICE CAKE

Ingredients:

2 cups granulated sugar
1 box seeded raisins
1 tablespoon cinnamon
1 teaspoon cloves
2 cups water
1 cup margarine
1 teaspoon nutmeg
4 cups flour
1 tablespoon baking soda
1/4 teaspoon salt
1 egg, beaten
1 cup water
1 cup chopped pecans (optional)

Directions:

Boil together sugar, raisins, cinnamon, cloves, 2 cups water, margarine and nutmeg for 10 minutes, then set aside to cool. Sift together flour, baking soda and salt. Add to boiled mixture. When cool, add beaten egg and 1 cup water. Stir in 1 cup chopped pecans, if desired. Bake in a greased and floured, 10-inch tube pan for 1 hour and 10 minutes in a 350°F oven.

Serves: 12

QUICK BLUEBERRY CHEESECAKE

Ingredients:

1 cup graham cracker crumbs
3 tablespoons butter or margarine, melted
3 (8 ounce) packages cream cheese, room temperature
3/4 cup sugar
3 eggs
1 teaspoon vanilla
1 cup blueberry pie filling

Directions:

Mix crumbs and butter or margarine. Press into a 9-inch pie pan. Set aside. Combine cream cheese and sugar. With mixer, mix 2 minutes on medium setting. Add eggs and vanilla. Mix 3 minutes more. Pour into crust. Bake at 450°F for 12 minutes. Reduce heat to 350°F and bake for 30 minutes more. Cool, and spoon blueberry filling over top.

Serves: 8

RED CAKE

Ingredients:
1/2 cup shortening
1 1/2 cup sugar
2 eggs
1 tablespoon cocoa
1/2 teaspoon salt
2 cups flour
1 1/4 cup buttermilk
1 teaspoon vanilla
1/2 teaspoon almond
   flavoring
1 tablespoon vinegar
1 teaspoon baking soda
Few drops of red food
   coloring

Directions:
Cream shortening, sugar and eggs until light and fluffy. Sift cocoa, salt, flour and baking soda together and add to egg mixture, alternately, with buttermilk and vinegar. Add vanilla and almond flavoring, and several drops of red food coloring. Pour into a greased 13 x 10 x 2 inch pan. Bake at 325°F for 40 minutes, or until done.

Serves: 12

WHITE CHERRY OR PECAN COOKIE

Ingredients:
1/2 pound margarine
3/4 cup confectioner's
   sugar
1 egg
2 cups flour
1 teaspoon vanilla
3 dozen candied
   cherries or pecans

Directions:
Mix ingredients in the order listed and drop by teaspoonfuls onto cookie sheet. Place cherry or pecan in center. Bake for 12 minutes at 350°F.

Serves: Makes 3 dozen

PIZZA PARFAIT PIE

Ingredients:
Crust:
2 cups sifted all-
  purpose flour
1/2 cup sugar
1/2 cup butter
1 egg, slightly beaten
Filling:
1 (3 ounce) package
  lime gelatin
1 1/4 cups hot water
1 pint vanilla ice cream
Topping:
2 medium-sized firm
  ripe bananas
3 tangerines, peeled and
  segmented
1 cup red grapes,
  halved
5 maraschino cherries,
  halved
24 small pecan halves

Directions:
For crust: sift flour and sugar into a medium-sized bowl; cut in butter. Stir in egg until pastry holds together. Press evenly over bottom and up sides of a 14-inch pizza pan; flute edge. Using fork, poke holes all over pie shell. Bake in moderate oven (375°) for 15 minutes, or until golden. Cool completely in pan on a wire rack. *For filling:* dissolve gelatin in hot water in a medium-sized bowl; stir in ice cream, a big spoonful at a time, until completely melted. Pour mixture into cooled pastry shell. Chill until firm. *For topping:* just before serving, peel bananas and slice diagonally. Arrange in rows over the filling to divide into four sections. Fill in sections with rows of tangerine segments, and rings of grapes, cherries and pecans. Cut into wedges.

Serves: 16

SESAME SEED COOKIES

Ingredients:
2 cups sugar
2 1/2 cups butter or
  margarine
6 eggs
2 teaspoons vanilla
1 teaspoon salt
8 cups flour
6 teaspoons baking
  powder
2 pounds sesame seeds

Directions:
Cream sugar and butter or margarine. Add eggs, beating well. Add salt and vanilla. Beat well and then beat in baking powder and flour. Spread sesame seeds onto a cutting board. Roll out dough on the board, into the seeds. Slice diagonally. Bake at 350°F for 12 minutes.

Serves: Makes 2 dozen

SMALL RAISIN CAKES

Ingredients:

2 cups water
1 1/2 cup sugar
1 cup shortening
1 cup raisins
1 egg, beaten
1 teaspoon cinnamon
1 teaspoon ground
   cloves
2 teaspoons baking soda
3 cups flour

Directions:

Bring to a boil the water, sugar, shortening, raisins, cinnamon and cloves, and cook for 20 minutes. Let stand until cold. Then mix in the egg, the 3 cups of flour, and baking soda. Pour into muffin pans that have been lined with paper cups. Bake at 350°F for 30 minutes.

Serves: Makes about 2 dozen

SPICY APPLESAUCE CAKE

Ingredients:

1 stick margarine
1 cup sugar (scant)
2 tablespoons water
   (hot water if apple-
   sauce is thick)
2 cups flour
2 teaspoons baking soda
1/4 teaspoon salt
2 cups applesauce
1/2 cup raisins
1/2 cup nuts
Dashes of cinnamon
   and nutmeg

Directions:

Mix all ingredients together. Bake in a greased and floured, standard-sized loaf pan at 350°F for 1 hour.

Serves: 10

SOUR CREAM CAKE

Ingredients:

Batter:
- 1/2 pound butter
- 2 cups sugar
- 4 eggs
- 2 cups sour cream
- 2 teaspoon baking soda
- 2 teaspoon baking powder
- 1 teaspoon vanilla
- 1/2 teaspoon salt
- 3 cups flour

Mixture:
- 1/2 cup sugar
- 2 teaspoons cinnamon
- 1 cup chopped nuts

Directions:

Mix together all batter ingredients. In a separate bowl, mix together the mixture ingredients. In a 10-inch tube pan, alternate layers of batter and mixture. Bake at 350°F for 55 minutes to 1 hour.

Serves: 12

STRAWBERRY SPONGE CAKE

Ingredients:
6 eggs, separated, at room temperature
1 cup sugar
Pinch salt
3/4 teaspoon cream of tartar
1 cup flour
2 quarts strawberries (save a few for garnish or add additional pint)
2 large and 1 small container of non-dairy whipped topping

Directions:
Beat egg whites, salt and cream of tartar until stiff. Set aside. Beat egg yolks and sugar until thick. Add to egg whites. Gently fold in flour. Bake in 2 (8-inch), pans for 20 to 30 minutes. Cool for 5 minutes, then remove cakes from pans. Slice each cake horizontally to make 4 cakes. Wash strawberries and remove stems. Cut into quarters and drain well. Add 1 large and 1 small container of non-dairy whipped topping and mix well. Set aside. Layer cakes, alternating with strawberry-topping mixture. End with cake. Then ice sides and top of cake with the remaining topping. Garnish with strawberries. Refrigerate cake. *Helpful Hints:* Cake slices best when made the night before and refrigerated overnight.

Serves: 8

STRAWBERRY PARFAIT

Ingredients:
1 small package strawberry gelatin
1 pint vanilla ice cream
1 package (frozen) strawberries
1 1/2 cups strawberries, sliced
1 small container whipped topping (optional)
Whole strawberries for garnish (optional)

Directions:
Mix gelatin with hot water, as directed on package. Add ice cream and let it melt into the gelatin. Add sliced strawberries to mixture and pour mixture evenly into 8 parfait glasses. Refrigerate. Garnish, if desired, with whipped topping and/or whole berries. Chill.

Serves: 8

STRAWBERRY SWIRL

Ingredients:
- 1 cup graham cracker crumbs
- 1/4 cup butter or margarine, melted
- 2 tablespoons sugar
- 2 cups sliced, fresh strawberries
- 1 (3 ounce) package strawberry-flavored gelatin
- 1 cup boiling water
- 1/2 pound marshmallows
- 1/2 cup milk
- 1 cup whipping cream, whipped

Directions:
Mix crumbs and melted butter or margarine and press into 9 x 9 x 2 inch baking dish. Chill. Sprinkle 2 tablespoons sugar over fresh berries. Let stand 1/2 hour. Dissolve gelatin in boiling water. Drain strawberries, reserving juice. Add water to juice to make 1 cup. Add to gelatin and chill until partially set. Meanwhile, combine marshmallows and milk. Heat (but do not boil) and stir until marshmallows melt. Cool thoroughly, then fold in whipped cream. Add berries to gelatin, then swirl in marshmallow mixture. Pour into crust and chill to set. Cut into squares.

Serves: 9-12

SUNNY BANANA PIE

Ingredients:
- 1 (9-inch) graham cracker crust
- 3 bananas
- 2 cups milk
- 1 (8 ounce) cream cheese, softened
- 1 package vanilla instant pudding mix
- 1 cup heavy cream, whipped

Directions:
Slice 2 bananas into crust. Gradually add 1/2 cup milk to softened cream cheese, mix well until blended. Add pudding mix and remaining milk. Beat slowly for 1 minute. Pour into crust. Chill. Garnish with banana slices and whipped cream.

Serves: 6

TINA'S CHOCOLATE FUDGE

Ingredients:

2 (3 ounce) packages cream cheese, room temperature

2 tablespoons butter or margarine

1 pound box confectioner's sugar

4 ounces unsweetened chocolate, melted

1/2 teaspoon vanilla

Directions:

With mixer on medium setting, mix cream cheese, 1/2 of butter or margarine and sugar. After 1 minute, add chocolate and vanilla. Mix thoroughly. Coat bottom of 9 x 9 x 2 inch pan with remaining butter or margarine. Pour mixture into pan and chill 45 minutes.

Serves: Makes 3 dozen 2 1/4-inch squares

PEACH PIE

Ingredients:

Filling:
1 (8 ounce) package cream cheese
2 tablespoons milk
1/4 teaspoon almond extract
2 tablespoons sugar
2 (10 ounce) packages frozen peaches, thawed
1 9-inch pastry shell, baked

Glaze:
1 tablespoon cornstarch
1/4 cup sugar
1 tablespoon lemon juice
2/3 cup peach juice
1 tablespoon margarine

Directions:

For filling: combine cream cheese, milk, almond extract and sugar. Mix well and spread into baked pastry shell. Chill. Drain peaches, reserving juice, arrange slices on cream cheese. *For glaze:* combine the 1 tablespoon cornstarch and 1/4 cup sugar in saucepan. Add 1 tablespoon lemon juice and 2/3 cup peach juice, stirring over medium heat till clear and thick. Add 1 tablespoon margarine and cook 2 minutes. When cool, pour over the peaches.

Serves: 6

VIENNA CHOCOLATE ICING

Ingredients:
4 squares unsweetened chocolate
1 cup confectioner's sugar
2 tablespoons hot water
2 eggs
6 tablespoons butter, softened

Directions:
Melt the unsweetened chocolate in double boiler. Add 1 cup confectioner's sugar and 2 tablespoons hot water and blend thoroughly. Add 2 eggs, one at a time, and beat briskly and thoroughly after each egg. Add 6 tablespoons butter, 2 tablespoons at a time, and beat well after each addition. Spread generously over a layer cake.

Serves: Frosts one cake

RICE PUDDING

Ingredients:

2 eggs, separated
1/2 cup sugar
2 cups milk
1 cup cooked rice
1 tablespoon butter, melted
1/2 cup raisins (more if desired)
2 tablespoons confectioner's sugar
1/8 teaspoon nutmeg

Directions:

Beat the egg yolks and mix in the granulated sugar and milk. Stir into the rice. Mix in the butter and raisins. Pour into a buttered, 1-quart baking dish. Beat the egg whites until frothy and beat in the confectioner's sugar. Spread on top of rice mixture. Sprinkle with nutmeg. Bake 325°F about 30 minutes.

Serves: 8

INDEX